Catholics Divorce & Remarriage

Father John Hosie s.m. is a Marist Father who has been working among the divorced and widowed and in relationship counseling for over twenty years.

He was an advocate for the Catholic Marriage Tribunal of Sydney for eight years.

He is the National Chaplain for the Catholic organization, Solo Parents of Australia. In 1979, he helped bring The Beginning Experience to Australia and New Zealand, and in 1985, the program, Rainbows for All God's Children.

Father Hosie is in charge of the History faculty at the Catholic Theological Union, Hunters Hill NSW.

Catholics Divorce & Remarriage

A frank look at a subject that affects many Catholics deeply

John Hosie S.M.

E.J. DWYER

The text of this book first appeared in *Annals Australia*, April–October, 1990, as a series of articles.

First published in booklet form in 1991 by
Chevalier Press
1 Roma Avenue
Kensington NSW 2033

This edition published in 1993 by
E.J. Dwyer (Australia) Pty Ltd
3/32–72 Alice Street
Newtown NSW 2042 Australia
Phone: (02) 550-2355
Fax: (02) 519-3218

National Library of Australia
Cataloguing-in-Publication data

Hosie, John, 1931–
Catholics, divorce & remarriage.

New ed.
Bibliography.
Includes index.
ISBN 0 85574 349 2.

1. Marriage — Australia — Religious aspects — Catholic Church.
2. Divorce — Australia — Religious aspects — Catholic Church. I. Title. II. Title: Catholics, divorce and remarriage.

248.8460994

Copy-edited by Ian Tonkin
Cover design by Warren Penney
Text design by Katrina Rendell
Typeset in 11/13 Garth Graphic by Sun Photoset Pty Ltd, Brisbane
Printed in Australia by Australian Print Group, Maryborough, Vic.

10 9 8 7 6 5 4 3 2 1
97 96 95 94 93

Distributed in Canada by:
Meakin and Associates
Unit 17
81 Auriga Drive
NEPEAN, ONT K2E 7Y5
Ph: (613) 226 4381
Fax: (613) 226 1687

Distributed in Ireland and the U.K. by:
Columba Book Service
93 The Rise
Mount Merrion
BLACKROCK CO. DUBLIN
Ph: (01) 283 2954
Fax: (01) 288 3770

Distributed in the United States by:
Morehouse Publishing
871 Ethan Allen Highway
RIDGEFIELD CT 06877
Ph: (203) 431 3927
Fax: (203) 431 3964

To

so many of my dearest friends who are divorced, separated and widowed: Thanks for your courage and example and love.

Contents

Introduction

Divorce is about defeat and failure. But it can also be about victory and success. It is about pain and grief and guilt, and also about healing and forgiveness and peace. It is about rejection. It can also be about acceptance. It is about the loss of hopes and the end of dreams. It can also be about new life, new hopes and new dreams. Often it is about continuing grief over children who are always separated from one parent or the other, and who doubt that they are part of a family any more. It can also be about pride in children who are more mature and more together than their peers, and about single-parent homes which are more united, more peaceful and more loving than many two-parent homes.

In a word, divorce is about death, but it can also be about resurrection.

It seems incredible to me that any Christian church could fail to see Christ in the divorced. And yet I am aware that one of the greatest pains for Catholics who are divorced has been the message they have received that there is no place for them in the Catholic church.

In trying to maintain its commitment to the ideal which

Jesus Christ put before us, the indissolubility of marriage, we lost sight of the reality: all of us fail; and all of us need pardon and forgiveness. It was to the outcasts, to people who had failed, that Christ offered his special love and compassion. He showed little respect for the Pharisees. When we, as a church, have made outcasts of people who may be more the victims of divorce than its champions, who are the Pharisees?

What Christ offered to us, by his word and example, was the promise that we, too, can overcome death as he did, and live again, and love again.

The chapters which follow first appeared as a series of articles in *Annals Australia* during 1990, and I am grateful to the editor, Father Paul Stenhouse MSC, for his valuable support in making them available to a wider public, then and now. I have some awareness of the need—I cannot count the hours I have spent listening to divorced people. The themes of the chapters were developed from formal or informal talks which, over a number of years, I had been asked to give to groups of the divorced.

Their messages to me all too often included the self-doubting questions: What happens to me now? Does the church care about me any more?

Many divorced Catholics have erroneous ideas about church teaching. Sadly, some believe—quite wrongly—that by simply being divorced, they became disqualified from receiving Holy Communion. Rarely can they grasp clearly what an annulment is, and because they took their marriage vows sincerely, they feel doubtful whether they could ever qualify for one.

If they remarry without an annulment, the ceremony is not recognized by the church, and they believe—equally wrongly, as we shall see—that they are excommunicated. Despite their unchanged religious beliefs, they think that they have lost their membership of their church, and would never be able to receive Holy Communion without leaving the new spouse, and perhaps breaking up a new family. Most of these ideas have been with them since childhood.

Many complain that they have difficulty in finding explanations of Catholic church teaching about divorce which they can follow. The exact Catholic position on these issues, as this book seeks to show, is more compassionate than many of us realize.

While the church has an unchanged commitment to the permanence of marriage, many Catholics are unaware that it now has a very different approach to divorced people themselves—an approach which could hardly be better expressed than in *When Dreams Die*, a very caring statement issued by the bishops of two countries. It may be read in Appendix I.

It is my hope that the following chapters will be helpful to these divorced people. The success of the first edition of this book and a thick file of correspondence reassure me that a wider audience is finding the information valuable. Close relatives of those who are divorced also have a need and right to know what the church does teach on these matters.

Sometimes parents make the sad decision to refuse to attend a remarriage ceremony of a daughter or son, and perhaps even to cut themselves off from their grandchildren because they believe that loyalty to the church requires them to do so. They may be helped by reading these pages.

Many who are widowed know that the church's laws on divorce do not apply to them in the sense that they would be free to remarry in the Catholic church if they chose to. But in time they could find themselves contemplating remarriage with a partner who is divorced:

suddenly the church's teachings on the subject may become very relevant indeed, to them.

Catholic schools today try to offer a much more realistic religious education program to their students. The pages which follow may assist class discussions on the subjects covered, enabling them to be, at the same time, compassionate and soundly based.

But more importantly, I hope that students will reach a determination that when the time comes for them to marry, they will give excellent preparation to their marriage, especially in the area of communication. As our bishops remind us in *When Dreams Die*, the divorced are often the best witnesses to the true meaning of marriage.

John Hosie s.m.
St Patrick's Presbytery
PO Box N 87
Grosvenor Place NSW 2000

CHAPTER 1

Understanding Marriage Breakdown

The last half century has seen a tragic increase in marriage breakdown throughout the world. It was rarely headlined. It was not spoken about very much. Unlike other tragedies—the road toll, for instance—politicians did not take it up as a vote-winning crusade. There were no public campaigns launched, no attempts to target and reduce contributing causes of the problem, as drunken driving has been targeted.

But tens of thousands more lives have been shattered by divorce than were ever affected by car smashes, and the number of divorces has risen tragically. The rewriting of divorce laws in many countries over recent years has seen the "no-fault" concept widely embraced. Often this has resulted in a court process in which the divorce itself takes less than five minutes. The floodgates opened.

Today, in the 1990s, about fifty per cent of marriages in the United States fail. In Canada the figure is a little over forty per cent; in the United Kingdom, Australia and New Zealand the numbers range between one marriage in three and forty per cent. More recently the rate of divorce in some of these countries leveled, only to rise again as a worldwide recession put new pressures on marriages. At the same time the average age at which men and women marry has been rising markedly.

In those countries with lower rates of first-marriage failures, the failure rate of *second* marriages where one or both partners had been married previously, has been rising more dramatically. The failure rate of the new marriages of those who remarry within a year of divorce is much higher: more than three out of four in several of those countries; overall about one in two fail. In the United States, where there are children the remarriage failure rate is around sixty per cent.

Past Catholic Attitudes

Among Catholics in the past, it was as if divorce did not exist. Admitting that a member of the family was divorced carried shame similar to that felt when a family member had been convicted of a crime and was in prison.

For ages, the only time we heard from the official church about divorce was once a year when the priest spoke about it from the pulpit, often describing it as "a cancer on family life." No doubt the purpose of this was to try to strengthen marriage and counter divorce. It had the unfortunate effect of leading many Catholics to believe that divorce was sinful. This is wrong: we shall see in a later chapter, on the authority of Pope John Paul II himself, that *divorce is not a sin*, and never was, even though the church opposed it.

Catholics in the past were aware that some rare people obtained an *annulment* of marriage, but hardly anyone knew any person who had done so. The priest assured us that an annulment meant that the church had declared that there had been "no marriage at all."

The grounds for annulment were also rare: *non-consummation*—meaning that the couple had never had intercourse, and could prove it; *forced marriage*—even more difficult to prove, where the person who married was pressured to do so (by parents, for instance) and under such duress that it could be said freedom was lacking.

Apart from those rare situations, the only easy annulments were for marriages involving a Catholic who had broken church rules by marrying "outside the church": in a registry office or in a religious ceremony which the Catholic church did not recognize.

But as the 1970s continued, divorce, which had been rare among Catholics, became common. The rate of divorce among Catholics in many countries now does not appear to be very different from that in the community generally. Most Catholics today have at least one close relative who is divorced. Very many of those people have entered a second marriage.

But some things did not change much. At least until recently, a divorced Catholic has usually felt rejected by the church, by family and friends. Clear messages were often given: "This has never happened in our family; you have let us all down." This was almost always accompanied by a feeling of *self-rejection* which is even harder to bear: "I've failed. Now I am one of *them*."

No one likes to feel an outcast, but little or no help was available. Thankfully these things are changing to some extent. Bishops in a number of countries have spoken out either individually or as a national body to express understanding and offer reassurance to the divorced. *When Dreams Die* is outstanding among such pastoral statements. It speaks in a very compassionate way to the divorced, and can be read in full in Appendix I. But there was, and often still is, a failure to communicate to the divorced any sense of understanding their situation.

Yet the unfortunate effects of marriage breakdown are many and serious. There is the inexpressible pain, for instance, of being a parent (usually, but not always a father) and losing custody—and no longer having daily contact with one's own children.

Real poverty is another effect. Studies of poverty in a number of countries continue to show that one of the largest groups falling below the poverty line consists of families led by a divorced mother.

I know one such mother, with pre-school children, who was removed from the list of part-time relief teachers in the local Catholic school at the order of her parish priest, because she was divorced. I feel ashamed that a priest could deprive her of income. I cannot see how he could reconcile that action with his conscience, but he probably thought he was doing something to counteract "the evil of divorce." Fortunately, she was able to obtain occasional work in other Catholic parishes which took a more Christian attitude.

Few except those who have been divorced really appreciate that it is one of the worst experiences that can happen to anyone. Its effects of grief are quite comparable to those felt at the death of a spouse. Added to those feelings can be a sense of failure, shame, guilt and anger which can be overwhelming. The divorced feel that they are drowning, and no one seems to know or care.

People whose marriages have ended may be in a state of shock for a long time. They may sit for hours staring at a blank wall. They often cannot concentrate at work. They lock the house or the car with the keys inside. They may unexpectedly find tears streaming uncontrollably down their face. They shout and scream at their children over trivial misdeeds. They set off in the car and suddenly realize they are driving in the wrong direction. They make rash, irrevocable and sometimes stupid decisions, such as to quit their job, or sell up everything and move to another state.

They say that many former close friends do not come near them any more. Those who do remain in contact seem unable to understand or to help, and the divorced sometimes make irrationally harsh, cutting comments to the very ones who are standing by them. Friends often attempt to "matchmake" the separated or divorced person with a partner on social occasions.

Unfortunately, divorced persons may be highly vulnerable. They may find themselves involved in "one-night stands," when they have never behaved promiscuously in their lives before. They may enter a relationship which leads to a completely unsuitable second marriage—and another divorce easily results, which is even more painful and seems to provide unwelcome proof of their inadequacy.

Judith Wallerstein, an American psychologist, in trailblazing research, followed up the long-term effects of divorce on a large number of families, and in her book *Second Chances: Men, Women and Children A Decade After Divorce* reports that ten years after divorce, in only ten per cent of the breakups were *both* of the former spouses living happier lives.

There is a positive aspect to all this. Some things have improved. There is now a great deal of knowledge of the grief process generally, and in particular, its effects upon marriage breakdown. If divorced persons want to, they can find very effective programs to help deal with grief, and achieve healing after the trauma of divorce. They can become better persons than they were before it happened.

Peer Ministry Support

Unfortunately, partly through ignorance about what help is available, only a minority of divorced spouses at present take part in such programs. It should be emphasized that reading a book is not normally enough. Peer ministry programs are needed: those who have experienced the failure of a marriage offer help to each other.

The Beginning Experience runs a live-in weekend which helps the divorced—or widowed—come to terms with the end of the marriage. It is now widely available in English-speaking countries, and some others. I recommend it without reservation. It can usually be contacted through the local Catholic welfare agency, and an international address is listed in Appendix II.

Some Catholic parishes now offer very helpful Support Group or Coping Programs which run for six or more weeks. These programs need minimal help (such as from *The Beginning Experience*) to set up, and can then be organized by a parish pastoral assistant, for instance, to continue without further outside help.

Similar work can also be done with a counselor experienced in the work, provided that the divorced person persists with sessions for as long as is needed.

Children

The effects of divorce on children can be traumatic. Some have claimed that the children get over the breakup after a year or two. These claims have been based on research which is too brief. Judith Wallerstein, referred to above, found that ten years after the marriage breakup, 35 per cent of the children had poor relations with *both* parents, many were clinically depressed, and no fewer than 40 per cent were coping with life poorly. Only 45 per cent were doing well. On the whole, parents fared better than children.

The best program for children I know of is called *Rainbows* and is run mostly within schools. It, too, is a peer ministry program. With a trained, sympathetic adult, over a period of about three months the children, teenagers or young adults, in small groups of about five, work through and learn to understand what has happened to them. *Rainbows* is written for students at every level from kindergarten to Higher School Certificate and beyond. The program is not therapy—it is for those who are coping. Those who need therapy should receive counseling from qualified people.

The *Rainbows* program is also widely available in the English-speaking world and information can be obtained at the contact address given in Appendix III.

In other words, although little help was available in the past, those affected by divorce can find help today in many places, and the situation is improving.

Questions for Discussion

1. "Divorce is a cancer on family life." Discuss.
2. Why do sole-parent homes make up such a high proportion of people who suffer from poverty?
3. A divorced person says, "I feel angry all the time." Discuss.
4. "Divorce is pretty hard on the children, but they get over it in a year or two." Discuss.

Questions for Discussion

CHAPTER 2

Annulments

We have seen that marriage breakdowns have massive effects on those involved. Although many go through a time of hurt when they express doubts about ever remarrying, the time may come when they change their minds, and would like to marry again.

In fact, a high proportion of people whose marriages have ended do remarry—up to 70 or 80 per cent. As with most general statistics, it does not seem that the figures for Catholics are much different from those of the general community.

Catholic church law (called Canon Law) permits a second marriage only if an *annulment* has been granted to the first marriage. This is required when a divorced Catholic wishes to remarry, or when a Catholic wishes to marry a person who has been married already. In the latter instance, in other words, divorced people who are not Catholics but wish to marry a Catholic may (and a number do) petition the Catholic marriage tribunal for a marriage annulment.

Some people believe that an annulment is a "Catholic divorce." It is not. In most English-speaking countries, a divorce is simply a recognition that one partner of a marriage no longer wishes to be married to the other (whether the other likes it or not). There are people who just "walk out" on a marriage, abandoning the partner (and children). The motive may be completely trivial—they may be bored with marriage or may have found a partner they think more attractive. In many of these countries, after a period of separation, such a person can obtain a divorce *no matter what the former partner thinks*. No "defense" is possible.

This is far from the meaning of an annulment. An annulment is a declaration by the church that what appeared to be a valid marriage was defective in some way regarded as *essential for the nature of a true marriage*. This declaration is made by a diocesan church body called the marriage tribunal.

A question which is often asked about annulments is, "If I get an annulment of my marriage, does that mean that my children would become illegitimate?" The answer, in a word, is "No." On this matter Catholic law parallels civil law, in which, if a person married in one city, and then, without getting a divorce, married again in another and had children, the second marriage could be *annulled* as bigamous. However, the children of that second marriage would still be considered legitimate, because it was presumed to be a valid marriage: the technical term is that it was a "putative" marriage. The same rule applies in Catholic church law where an annulment is granted.

Presumed Valid

The church has an initial presumption that all marriages which have taken place according to the rules are valid.

Most Catholics are well aware that any marriage in the Catholic church is presumed by the church to be valid. But some Catholics express surprise to learn that the Catholic church has a similar presumption about the first marriages of people who are not Catholic, whether theirs was a church or a civil marriage.

But a moment's reflection shows that the Catholic church could take no other attitude: it would be insulting to other people to suggest that the only valid marriages are those of the Catholic church, and that married members of other churches (or married people with no religion) are not truly married.

Two exceptions to this presumption of validity deserve mention: the church does not recognize a marriage where a Catholic was involved who was *not obeying Catholic church law*; nor does it recognize any marriage to a person who has been divorced. If a person—Catholic or not—who had been in such a marriage was divorced, the Catholic church would quickly recognize their freedom to remarry in a Catholic ceremony.

Suppose, for example, that Mike, a Catholic, wishes to marry Judy, a Lutheran; but Judy was previously married to Jim. If that first marriage of Judy and Jim took place in the registry office, and Jim was a Catholic—and therefore not obeying church rules—or if Jim had been married previously, once the facts were established, the Catholic church would quickly recognize that Judy is free to marry Mike.

Such instances aside, an annulment process is a lengthy business. But it should be mentioned that very many Catholics, and some priests, have misapprehensions about the *grounds* on which annulments are granted.

Misunderstandings

Some people do not apply for an annulment because they believe that they would be asked to declare that they "didn't really mean it" when they took their marriage vows. In fact, it must be rare for a person to marry with this frame of mind, and it would be difficult to convince a tribunal that such was the case. I do not know anyone who married without wanting it to succeed.

A similar misunderstanding is revealed when you hear someone say, "How could I get an annulment? I have three children." Their ideas go back to the time when annulments were very rare, and non-consummation—not having had sexual intercourse—was one of the few grounds people were aware of.

When considering whether they could gain an annulment in the Catholic church for a marriage which has ended in divorce, people should seek expert advice from someone familiar with current tribunal practice—not the hazy ideas of a friend, or even a priest not sure of current practice. It is quite all right for a divorced Catholic to contact the Catholic Marriage Tribunal of the diocese and say, "I would like to find out if I have grounds for an annulment."

Not Expected to Know

It is important to note that such people are not expected to come to the tribunal already knowing and able to state the grounds on which they hope to get an annulment. These grounds have technical names and, in any event, there might be two or even three possible lines on which a case might proceed, depending on the available evidence. They are invited to make an appointment with a tribunal representative without knowing whether they have grounds or not, or what the grounds might be, and are very welcome.

Some people say that they do not want to seek an annulment because it would mean declaring that "There was no marriage at all." This phrase can be misleading and is not very helpful. People say: "I have four children to prove there was one." They need to know that a decree of nullity declares that the marriage was not valid because something was lacking which ought to be present in a marriage, and that it does not question the legitimacy of the children. "The marriage was invalid" is accurate, and less disturbing.

When they hear that the annulment process requires applicants to take a very close look at their own life and the marriage, many people say, "But that would be very painful." They are right: it is painful. But all people whose marriages have failed need to make an "agonizing reappraisal," to use a famous phrase—whether they do it or not (and most do not), and whether they seek an annulment or not. They need to look deeply at their life and marriage, even though it is painful to do so.

This is pain which cannot be avoided. The price of not doing so is likely to be a failed second marriage. An annulment process is one way in which this reappraisal can be made.

Grounds

The grounds on which the church grants annulments were extended considerably some years ago to include psychological causes.

A simple example will perhaps best reveal the contrast between past and present tribunal practice. Suppose that two Catholics were married in a Catholic ceremony, and even though they had a child or two, it became clear that one was homosexual: they separated and were divorced. For many years until relatively recently, no annulment would have been granted by the Catholic church: the marriage was seen as sacramental and consummated—sexual intercourse had taken place.

But today, the tribunal would accept the case: it would be argued that a homosexual person does not have the *capacity* to commit himself or herself to marriage which is, of its nature, a heterosexual state of life: an annulment could be granted.

Another obvious example is what we usually call *immaturity*; its technical name as a ground for annulment is "lack of due discretion." Civil laws in all countries declare that persons under a certain age are not able to marry validly. In most English-speaking countries, a girl of fifteen who went through a marriage ceremony successfully pretending to be eighteen could be granted a civil annulment—an annulment, not a divorce.

All countries have laws recognizing that persons of a certain age—such as eighteen—may legally marry without parental permission. But some of us are well aware that when we were eighteen, we were still very immature, to the degree that we would have been unready to take on the responsibilities of marriage. Immaturity is a rather vague term and all of us are immature in some ways, but in certain people this *serious* lack of maturity may persist for years. If a divorced person can establish to the marriage tribunal that when the marriage took place, one or other partner was seriously immature in the sense described, an annulment of the marriage could be granted.

Responsibilities

There are other grounds relating to the capacity of a person to undertake the responsibilities of marriage. Some people seem to be continually incapable of being faithful to their spouses; such marriages lack the necessary qualities of trust and fidelity. Some seem quite irresponsible in a range of ways as spouses, almost acting as if still single, and irresponsible as parents.

Other individuals, although married, may remain in such a state of *emotional dependence* upon parents that they fail regarding one of the qualities of marriage mentioned earliest in scripture: "This is why man leaves father and mother and joins himself to his wife" (Genesis 2:24).

Psychological characteristics which are revealed by addiction, such as to alcohol, drugs or gambling, are other instances which would be very relevant to a petition for nullity.

A person whose marriage began only because the woman was pregnant and they wanted to give the baby a name would also have possible grounds for a nullity petition.

These instances are not at all a full list of grounds, but only examples. A number of other grounds might also be pursued, and result in a successful application.

Divorce First

It should be noted that in some places, a petition to the tribunal can only begin after a divorce has been granted, and outstanding court actions completed (e.g. disputes over custody of children, or the property settlement).

Local councils of bishops sometimes impose such requirements seeking to avoid the risk that evidence from the church's tribunal could be used in civil actions.

When a person considering seeking an annulment has discussed the matter with someone who is familiar with tribunal practice, and decides to proceed, the major steps are as follows:

First a lengthy interview will be arranged with a tribunal representative. This is a private meeting. In fact, no kind of court appearance is required either of the petitioner or any witnesses. The case proceeds entirely by written statements, prepared after help from an interviewer. During the first interview, the nature of the annulment process is explained, and the interviewer asks the person to make a fairly thorough explanation of the marriage and its breakdown, to gain a preliminary idea of the likely grounds. If no clear grounds can be seen, the petitioner is given this information.

As a result of this interview, a lengthy statement is put together by the petitioner about the marriage, and the backgrounds of both of the former spouses. Further help may be obtained from the interviewer in the preparation of this statement, which is the basis of the case.

The second part of the process is that the petitioner is asked to name people ("witnesses") who would be prepared to be interviewed. These may include parents, close relatives and friends. If the former spouse is prepared to be interviewed, the progress of the case is likely to be easier. Without that cooperation, the case can still proceed, but may be more difficult. The witnesses are then invited to get in touch with the tribunal to be interviewed.

When witnesses have been interviewed, the grounds on which the case will proceed to judgment will be finally chosen on the basis of the petitioner's lengthy statement and the evidence of the witnesses. The grounds may primarily relate to the petitioner or to the former spouse, or may concern both as regards each other.

At a late stage, the petitioner is contacted again briefly to approve and sign the necessary application, and the case proceeds to judgment. If the judgment is favorable, it proceeds to a higher regional or national tribunal, and following on that body's approval, the annulment is granted.

Petitions which are not progressing usually drop out: the number actually refused is not as high as some imagine. Cases may be taken up again later if, for example, a witness becomes available. If refused, an appeal is possible, though not easy.

The petitioner is asked to contribute towards the cost of the process: the sum is usually comparable to the cost of a civil divorce petition.

Can an Annulment be Bought?

The accusation is sometimes made that annulments can be bought. No one could ever say that such a thing is impossible. However, in the twenty-five years since I first began working with people seeking an annulment, I have never come across even a suspicion that a case might have had an easier path if the petitioner was wealthy. By contrast, I have many times heard wealthy people complain that cases were too difficult. And if people are in difficult financial circumstances, cases proceed even though they may be able to afford only part of the cost—or none at all. I have known a number of people who were not at the time in a position to be able to pay the costs, and the annulment case has proceeded.

Unfortunately, annulments may take a good deal of time. A number of tribunals in the United States average six months for cases—and some take less time. Many other countries are much slower, however, aiming at completing cases in eighteen months, but they may take several years. The unavailability of witnesses and other factors can cause frustrating delays.

We noted above, however, that as many as 70 or 80 per cent of divorced people remarry.

What are the issues facing these people?

Questions for Discussion

1. What do you understand is meant by an annulment?
2. If the church or state grants an annulment of a marriage, does that mean that any children of the couple have become illegitimate?
3. "I've heard your church has marriage annulments. That's a Catholic divorce, isn't it?" Reply.
4. "There's no point in my applying for an annulment because I have no idea what grounds there could be for the application." Discuss.
5. A person says to you, "I have heard that all it takes to get a Catholic annulment is money paid to the right people." Reply.

CHAPTER 3

Remarriage

A high proportion of those who divorce enter another marriage. It would be expected that people "get it right" the second time.

Unfortunately, throughout the English-speaking world *the majority* of those who remarry do not get it right: more second marriages fail than succeed. Second marriages which take place within a year of the granting of a divorce have *a much greater chance of failing* than of succeeding.

These statistics ought to be well known. They ought to be headlined. Unfortunately they are not.

Words are inadequate to describe the tragic consequences of these second failures. Many people who have been divorced for a first time describe it as one of the worst experiences of their lives. Those who have had a *second* marriage fail often say it was far worse still than the first failure. Phrases like "two time loser" come accusingly into their minds.

The further disruptions to life and property are tragic. But as with the end of a first marriage, the most important tragedies will usually be the effects on children.

Why do second marriages fail? Statistics do not offer

explanations. However, it is clear that the great majority of divorced people do little or nothing to help themselves deal with the grief over the loss of the marriage. It is an area that a person should pay attention to before seriously contemplating a new relationship.

The belief that "Time heals all things" is not necessarily true. There are people who remain bitter and unhappy over a broken marriage for years and years. They do not have many friends because friends find it unpleasant to spend time with them: they will always start talking about how badly they were treated. When we see them coming we try to avoid them. Time has not healed them.

Most people cope with grief by trying not to think about it. At first this is necessary for survival. But as time passes and they are able to forget about it—most of the time—they may begin to believe that they have dealt with the grief. They have not. It remains inside.

Many try to escape or cover over grief feelings by rushing into a new relationship. This is avoidance, and will not work. The new relationship does occupy their attention greatly, but does nothing to heal the grief. Such a relationship can all too easily drift into a new marriage. The old phrase described this as "marriage on the rebound." It implied—correctly—that the person had not properly recovered from the loss of the old partner, and was not sufficiently stable for a decision about remarriage.

People may begin a new relationship for other inadequate reasons, such as to make the former spouse feel jealous, or to convince themselves that they are still attractive, or some such thing. This is a tragic way to use the new partner, and does not augur well for the relationship—yet it may drift into a remarriage.

Deal with Grief

Programs mentioned already, such as Support and Coping Programs, and *The Beginning Experience*, will help a person to close the door gently on a marriage which has ended. But *any divorced person who has not taken specific action towards dealing with grief ought to do so, even if the marriage ended some years previously.* When two people marry, each is always carrying emotional "baggage." Unresolved grief is baggage heavy enough to damage or even destroy the marriage.

There are other reasons for the failure of second marriages. Undoubtedly, the second marriages of many people fail for the *same reason* as their first marriages failed, whatever that was.

Some Marry the "Same" Person Again

In fact, a great many people marry a second spouse who is frighteningly like the first. Not physically alike, although it may happen. What matters are emotional resemblances: temperament, characteristics to do with dominance and submissiveness, those of people who act as helpless victims or show tendencies towards physical violence, people who are cold and unemotional, and those who can express their feelings easily, and so on.

American psychologist Harville Hendrix has researched widely to help people understand why, in the serious relationships of their lives, they choose particular types of partners.

Many times when counseling I found his theories borne

out. Once was when I was on talkback radio; the subject was divorce. A woman telephoned and said, "I'm not sure I qualify. I'm not phoning about a divorce, but about my long-term relationship which has just ended. But actually I was divorced a few years ago."

She paused for a moment and then said somewhat irrelevantly, "My friend was a very cold man ... As a matter of fact, my former husband was a very cold man, too."

"Do you like cold people?" I asked her. "Oh no!" she replied emphatically, "I like people who are warm and affectionate."

"Yet in two of the most important relationships of your life, you have chosen men who could not show affection," I said, "and it didn't work. Was there anyone like that in your childhood?"

"My mother," she answered at once. "She could never put her arms around us."

The frustrating thing with such conversations on talkback radio is that you never know whether callers do anything about their problem. Harville Hendrix would say that the woman probably craves affection, but was drawn towards men who resemble her mother in being unable to show it. Her hope is that one of them will change, and become warm and loving. It is not a very realistic hope.

I knew a man whose two failed marriages were to very motherly women. Each woman found that he was really looking for a mother, rather than a wife. He had lost his own mother when a young child, but he was unable to recognize this need within himself. Until he does so, he will keep being attracted to very motherly women, and continue the succession of marriage failures.

Until we recognize our motivations, we are likely to keep repeating our mistakes. We may say of a particular relationship that "It doesn't mean anything." But it is important to realize how easy it is for such a relationship to drift into a second marriage—which is very likely to fail.

What is needed, then, is for people to learn to understand themselves, and in particular to *recognize their part in the failed marriage.*

Solo Parents of Australia, a Catholic organization for the divorced and widowed, carried out a survey of its members in 1986 to look at the attitudes and experience of its members in a number of areas. A worryingly high number of answers suggested that the former spouse was entirely responsible for the failure of the marriage.

I say that this is worrying, because there has never been a failed marriage to which one person contributed 100 per cent of the failure, and the other was in no way responsible. Any who place all the blame on a former spouse are being blind to their own areas of responsibility for the failure of the marriage. If they can think of no other obvious possibilities, they could perhaps begin by asking themselves the question: "Why did I choose a partner with those characteristics?"

They will probably say that they had no idea that the person they were attracted to was like that, but an inner part of them did know, and this was part of the immediate attraction.

Special Preparation for Remarriage

Obviously, *specialized marriage preparation* is now needed within the community to assist people who are remarrying. But when two people have decided to get married, it may already be too late. A person who is divorced may have already chosen another unsuitable partner, because of not having sorted out the previous marriage and their own part in its failure.

For couples entering what will be a second marriage for either of them, there are areas of special need for preparation. Often there will be children involved, either living with them, and/or visiting during times of access, if they do not have custody. The new couple may have more children. There is much to be learnt beforehand.

There can be many possible variations of family situations, ranging from the difficulties of a person who has never been a parent acquiring an "instant family" on the one hand, to the problems of a step- or "blended" family combining two sets of children (at least occasionally) on the other.

Cartoonists often sum up problems brilliantly. One pictured a tumultuous family scene with an onlooker explaining: "His children and their children are fighting with her children."

Children place enormous pressure on any marriage. Much more so when they are loaded with inner anger over the loss of their original family. It is not easy to learn to be a successful step-parent—and the word still carries an unhappy tone. Step-parents attempting to discipline must learn to face the retort, "You can't tell me what to do. You're not my father (or mother)."

All parents have to learn to be fair to the child, but also to be united and supportive of each other in discipline expectations. Otherwise, children are able to drive a wedge between them—and they will always try!

"I thought I told you not to watch television."

"Dad said I could."

In a second marriage, unless the parents are very understanding and also united, it is even easier for a child to manipulate the natural parent against the step-parent, and cause problems which may trigger the breakdown of the new marriage.

Probably more than ninety per cent of the breakdowns of second marriages, where there are children, are triggered by the children. Note that this refers to the actual *trigger* of the breakdown: the *cause* is likely to be something lacking in the marriage at a more fundamental level.

How important it is, then, for the couple entering a second marriage to have as much help as possible, by way of specific preparation. This is not just something which concerns Catholics, but the community generally, as more and more children live in families with a parent and a step-parent. Yet the vast majority of marriage preparation organizations do not offer the special programs which should be available to prepare *couples entering second marriages.*

I have written at greater length about many of these issues in another book, *Before You Love Again: Starting a Successful New Relationship* (Millennium Books). For further details see the Bibliography.

There are problems which particularly concern Catholics in second marriages. Let us now turn our attention to those.

Questions for Discussion

1. How does the failure rate of second marriages compare with that of first marriages?
2. "My first marriage had no chance. My husband was an alcoholic. It wasn't my fault: I tried my best. There was nothing I could do about it." Discuss.
3. What do you think are some of the reasons why so many second marriages fail?

4. What effects do children have on second marriages?
5. How could the likelihood of a second marriage failure be reduced?

CHAPTER 4

Remarried Catholics and Holy Communion

Up to four out of five divorced people enter a second marriage. It would seem that the figures for Catholics are not greatly different.

Since the number of annulments granted annually is small, and there are thousands of remarriages, it is clear that only a very minor percentage of Catholics who remarry do so in a Catholic ceremony.

In other words, the vast majority of divorced Catholics who remarry do so in a civil marriage ceremony, or in a church of another denomination. The Catholic church does not officially recognize these marriages. A consequence is that it does not express any preference about where the ceremony takes place.

What is the status of these Catholics?

John Paul II

Our starting point is what the Pope has said. John Paul II issued a document in 1981 with the Latin title *Familiaris Consortio* on the subject of family life. In it he made it clear that divorced Catholics enjoy full and complete union with the church, they are not excommunicated, and may receive the Eucharist. In other words, the Pope makes it clear that *divorce is not a sin.* Sadly, a lot of Catholics are not aware of this.

He also spoke of Catholics who are divorced and remarried—his words would apply equally to a never-married Catholic who has married someone who was divorced. These Catholics, married "outside the church" as we usually say, should not, the Pope said, consider themselves as separated from the church, "for as baptized persons they can and indeed must share in its life." Once again, the Pope's words make it clear that they are *not excommunicated.*

But speaking in a general way he said that such Catholics may not participate in the Eucharist. The Pope urged them to seek an annulment of the first marriage—an annulment would help them become officially eligible.

What about the situation where an annulment is not possible? The Pope here summed up concisely the official teaching. But most Catholics in this situation are not aware that the church has always had what might be called a "second level" of teaching applying at the level of conscience, which is very relevant to them.

Thus John Paul spoke of those "who are sometimes subjectively certain in conscience that their previous and irreparably destroyed marriage had never been valid." However, he made no concessions as regards the status of their relationship as a marriage. The only way open to them to achieve a Catholic marriage is to bring that first marriage to the tribunal for annulment.

But the people he described include many whose marriages will never be annulled, not because their case is not a strong one, but because witnesses cannot be located, or refuse to be interviewed. Sometimes a key witness is dead. Does the church have anything to say to them?

Similarly, a Catholic married to a divorced person who is not a Catholic will, perhaps, have good reason to believe that an annulment could be granted to the first marriage of that partner—but the partner does not wish to apply to the tribunal.

There is little that the Catholic can do about it. The partner may say, very reasonably, "Look, if this annulment process only involved me, I would be happy to do it for you. But you tell me that it would mean asking friends, and my own parents, and even my ex-spouse to agree to be interviewed, and I don't think I want to do that." This attitude is perfectly understandable, no matter how anxious a Catholic partner might be for an annulment of that first marriage. Does the church have anything to say to them?

The conflict faced by a Catholic in either of these situations is knowing that it is very likely that the first marriage was not in itself binding in the sight of God, but this is not going to be able to be established officially.

Conscience Decision

The church does have something to say to such people. In such instances, the Catholic may make a decision in what is called the "internal forum," or a *conscience decision*, and may then continue to receive Holy Communion.

It should be emphasized that this is a perfectly correct moral principle, and is totally orthodox. It is not a case of people "making up their own rules." It was explicitly referred to in 1973 by the cardinal in charge of the church's highly authoritative teaching body in Rome called the Congregation for the Doctrine of the Faith.

In a letter dated 11.4.1973, which appears in the *Canon Law Digest*, 9:503f, Cardinal Seper urged pastors of souls to:

> follow up with special solicitude those who are living in an irregular union, applying in the solution of such cases, in addition to other correct means, the approved practice of the church in the internal forum.

In plainer English, the cardinal was saying that priests (and others) should take special care of people whose marriages are not recognized by the church and, in addition to other correct means [such as inviting them to seek an annulment of a previous marriage], should apply the church's *approved practice* of the good conscience solution. This could enable them to receive Holy Communion.

Pope John Paul certainly did not rule out this outcome in his reference, quoted above, to people who are objectively certain that their previous marriage was not valid.

Rules

There are rules applying to the conscience decision. They were spelt out two years after Cardinal Seper's letter by one of his successors, Archbishop Hamer, of the same Roman congregation.

Hamer said that those who use this solution should try to live good Christian lives, and should *avoid scandal* by receiving the sacraments where they are not known (*Canon Law Digest* 9:504f).

Scandal means behavior which is likely to lead another person into committing sin. It does not include the person who pretends to be shocked, and makes harsh judgments. That is called the scandal of the Pharisees—those whom Jesus described as hypocrites. We do not have to shape our behavior to please them.

Many people have no comprehension of how *any* marriage can be annulled and the person be allowed to remarry in the Catholic church. Theirs is not the kind of "scandal" which is warned against.

Finally note that scandal is not to be presumed. If the circumstances of a person's second marriage are not known generally (bearing in mind that there is no list which appear in newspapers of those who have been granted a marriage annulment), such remarried Catholics could certainly receive Holy Communion in the parish in which they live.

Another important point is that the conscience decision is one which the church expects people to take for themselves. They may, of course, obtain help—and such help ought to be available. In fact, Cardinal Seper placed the responsibility on priests and other "pastors of souls" to seek out such people and offer them this help. But in the end, the decision which the individual takes is not an official one—it applies at the level of conscience. They do not proceed on the basis that "Father X said it was all right."

Since the principles which the church tribunal applies in the granting of an annulment are not well understood generally, it is not easy for a Catholic in a second marriage which has taken place outside the church to reach such a decision about a previous marriage. Catholics have also long been used to being told NOT to make moral decisions on their own consciences. They often find it very difficult to take such an important step alone. But this is what the church asks.

The conscience decision is not based merely on a desire

to receive Holy Communion (although this desire obviously inspires the effort by people to look at their situation). Rather, it is based on a conviction that the first marriage was *not* one which ought to be seen as valid and binding, even though this will probably never be officially declared by the church.

Some find it regrettable that Catholics who have very cautiously and carefully taken a conscience decision about their second marriage, and are receiving Holy Communion, may be open to harsh judgment by other Catholics, and have no paper or document from the church to support them. But we can hope that in time people who are now unaware of the church's teachings on which such decisions are based will learn about them, and be less judgmental.

However, despite their fears, it is highly unlikely that there will ever be an embarrassing occasion in the church in which their status, which is correct in the sight of God, is going to be called into question. In fact, people whose remarriages have taken place with the church's blessing are virtually never asked to produce a certificate which shows this.

From another viewpoint, there is a positive side to the clear indications from the church that it wishes people to take a responsible moral decision in these situations which the marriage tribunal does not cover. They show that the church recognizes individual responsibility in a way which has moved a good distance from the attitude which was taught to many of us in our early years.

Prior to the Second Vatican Council Catholics were told that in making any serious moral decision, they ought to have permission in advance from the appropriate church authority, such as a confessor. Failing that, it should be brought to him as soon as possible afterwards, and checked.

The council took a new attitude in regard to conscience, its authority in our lives, and our obligation to follow its dictates. In the time before the council, it is difficult to think of a moral issue comparable in importance with the conscience decision, on which there was such clear and authoritative recognition by an official church body of the responsibility of the individual conscience.

I find that very many divorced Catholics, on hearing about these possibilities, supported by highest authorities in the church, are very happy, but they ask, "Why haven't I heard about this before?"

Inadequate Communication

Unfortunately, in the whole area of divorce, there has been a sadly inadequate communication by the church. I still meet Catholics who have not been to Holy Communion for years merely because they are divorced—unaware that nothing prevents them from receiving the sacrament, and the Pope has said so.

Perhaps there was an unstated belief that divorce was evil, and if we closed our eyes to it, it would go away. It is not going to go away, even though it is indeed a tragedy. It should be opposed as much as possible by prevention, including excellent preparation for marriage. It has not been decreased by making outcasts of those who have suffered the tragedy.

Rather than a lack of communication, what is needed is excellent communication. Undoubtedly, among remarried Catholics there are also people missing out on Holy Communion, and sometimes drifting away from the church, because they are unaware that they may be entitled to receive the sacraments.

Much is changing. We already mentioned a pastoral

letter, *When Dreams Die*, written by the bishops of New Zealand in the early 1980s. It was also released by Australia's bishops in their own name. It expresses a compassion for those who have suffered from the breakdown of marriage—a compassion which the divorced looked for in vain from the church in the past.

However, the words of Cardinal Seper quoted above do not merely indicate the possibility that those living in second marriages without an annulment may return to the sacraments. They also make it clear that pastors of souls have a *responsibility* to follow up these people with "special care": they should be welcomed and helped, not treated as outcasts.

We have been talking of those in second marriages who are convinced that a first marriage was not binding. Can anything be done to help a person who believes that the first marriage was valid? In the next chapter we will address this question.

Questions for Discussion

1. Is divorce a sin? Explain.
2. Someone says to you, "I always thought that a Catholic who remarries outside the church is excommunicated." Reply.
3. What is the *main basis* for a good conscience decision about receiving Holy Communion when in a second marriage?
4. If a person takes a *conscience decision* about a serious moral issue, what does it mean to "cause scandal"? Discuss.
5. Someone says to you, "I saw a Catholic going to Holy Communion and I know that the man she married was divorced; isn't that disgraceful?" Reply.

CHAPTER 5

Can a Marriage Die?

We have been looking at the situation of Catholics remarried without an annulment of a first marriage which they sincerely believe to be invalid. We have seen that a most authoritative church body has clearly indicated circumstances in which they may make a decision *in good conscience* and receive Holy Communion.

What is the situation of someone who believes that a first marriage was valid, or is at least uncertain?

Belief Is Not Proof

The first thing to note is that belief that a marriage was valid is not proof that it was valid. I have known divorced Catholics who were convinced that their marriage was valid, yet the former spouse applied for an annulment which was granted.

I am not implying that the tribunal decision was wrong: quite the reverse. I have always found our tribunals scrupulously careful in collecting solid evidence before granting annulments. If anything, they may be more careful than necessary in this regard. What I am saying is that the decision of the legally conservative tribunal clearly shows that a spouse was incorrect in believing that the marriage was valid.

This is not to imply that any marriage ending in divorce will have grounds for an annulment. Someone who simply became bored with being married and walked out on a spouse would not have grounds for annulment. But there would be no difficulty for such a person in obtaining a divorce: separation for a legally prescribed term is all that has to be proved.

Divorced people discussing the possibility of obtaining a marriage annulment will often say of their first marriage, "I always thought it was valid." Their conviction probably indicates no more than that they were genuine in pronouncing the vows of marriage, and sincerely intended that it would be until death.

However, though it may be unfounded, the belief of an average person that a first marriage was valid can make the difficulties in coming to a conscience decision seem immense. This is especially so when they have been brought up to consider that it was not right for a Catholic to make important moral decisions alone: they had to obtain permission from a priest. Yet now they are supposed to take responsibility for this major decision. They need informed help. It can be very difficult to find.

Not Easy to Understand

The annulment process is not easy to understand. In working among the divorced, I speak to many Catholics who have received annulments, who say to me, "I still can't say I really understand it." Many priests are not well informed about the current practices of the tribunal. How much more difficult it is, then, for lay people to *feel sure* of their grounds for believing that a first marriage—their own or that of their spouse—would be able to be declared invalid, if it could be submitted to the tribunal, and witnesses were available. Very many feel uncertain.

If such Catholics are to learn whether they might be entitled to receive the Eucharist, there is another concept which needs to be explained here. It concerns the general law of the church and what we might call the *objective status* of a Catholic remarried without an annulment of a previous marriage—their own, or that of their partner—as contrasted with the question of whether they are in sin *at a personal level.* Since it is an unfamiliar idea for any who are accustomed to different traditions based on English law, let me try to explain it.

Two Levels

Church law may operate at two levels: one—the objective, general level, and secondly the level of personal conscience. The presumption of law, for instance, is at the general level, and we saw from the words of Pope John Paul II that the presumption of law regarding marriage still stands: a marriage taking place according to the rules is presumed to be valid—unless or until an annulment is granted. His words indicate that the church unequivocally stands by its teaching that marriage, of its nature, is indissoluble.

But while he encouraged people to seek annulments, John Paul did *not* say that there are no circumstances under which a person could receive Holy Communion without an annulment, and he spoke compassionately to Catholics who are divorced and remarried.

When the Pope speaks officially in public, and in documents, it is usually at the objective, general level. Nevertheless, he can also speak at the personal level. Thus, he sometimes hears confessions at the Vatican: there he is able to speak at the second level of personal conscience without being misunderstood. This could include a discussion about the right of an individual remarried Catholic to receive Holy Communion, scandal being avoided.

The different approach of church law may be illustrated by an example. Technically, the church does not recognize divorce. But, as we noted, in a number of places the church *requires* Catholics to obtain a divorce *before* they can begin an annulment application. From English-based traditions of civil law, we might think that the people concerned are being asked to "break" the church's general law on the indissolubility of marriage, to enable the annulment case to proceed. Yet in church law this is not the case, and they are certainly *not* seen as being in a bad state of conscience.

Similarly, many people remarry (e.g. in a civil ceremony) before they obtain an annulment of a previous marriage. Until the annulment is granted their "objective status" does not fulfil those teachings of the church. However, it is interesting that once an annulment has been granted, and the remarriage is "blessed," the church regards the second marriage as having *begun*, not with the Catholic church's blessing, but when they pronounced their vows civilly—even though at that time their objective status was seen as not fulfilling the general law of the church about indissolubility.

An understanding of these concepts is relevant for many Catholics concerned about whether to apply for a divorce, or worrying because they remarried before annulment procedures were completed.

Return Not Possible

A separate point which deserves to be noted is that the Holy Father did not express a rule that divorced people should go back to a former spouse. In the vast majority of cases, reconciliation is a question which relates to the time before the final step of divorcing. For most people, there is simply no possibility of returning to the former spouse, especially if there is a second marriage. There may be obligations to a new spouse, and possibly children to the second marriage to consider.

In fact, any divorced person who carries an inner belief that the marriage will somehow revive may be in a state of mind which is very unhealthy, and damaging to their day-to-day life. I can recall a woman, divorced eight years, whose ex-husband had remarried and had a child in the new marriage. He virtually never contacted the children of his first marriage.

Something about the way she spoke about him made me ask: "Do you think that one day, the phone will ring, and he will say, 'I'm sorry. I was wrong. Can I come back?'"

She paused, and then said reluctantly, "Well . . . not soon."

Not Facing Reality

Retaining such a hope in the circumstances meant that she was not facing reality. It would be tragic indeed if she believed that she was being in some way "more

Catholic'' by refusing to recognize that the marriage was over. I wondered whether the very sad refusal of her former husband to contact his children had been affected by an awareness that she was likely to regard such contacts as ''proof'' that the failed marriage was going to start again.

The Beginning Experience, the Catholic program to help people come to terms with the end of a marriage, sees the process of recovery of a person from the grief of the end of a marriage in terms of ''Death and Resurrection.'' A person locked into impossible hopes of the revival of a marriage which has ended is in an unhealthy ''spiritual death'': lost, dead and without hope for the future. By facing the grief over the loss and closing the door on the painful past, they can begin to live again, and look to the future with renewed hope and confidence.

There were times when people in a second marriage, without an annulment, were described as ''living in sin,'' or were specifically accused of being in a *state of adultery*.

Adultery?

Such terms imply that the previous marriage in some way still exists, and that the rights of a former partner are continually being transgressed by the new marriage. They more probably relate to earlier definitions of marriage as a contract for the sexual generation of children. The *New Code of Canon Law*, basing itself on Vatican II, defines marriage as a covenant by which a man and woman establish between them a ''partnership of the whole of life'' (Canon 1055). The qualities of marriage emphasized by this and other recent official church statements are mutual love and faithfulness, rather than rights to sexual actions.

Such principles are the basis on which a number of theologians argue that a marriage can *die*. If two people are divorced, if the obligations arising from the marriage are discharged, and each is living a new life in a second marriage, these writers say that it is meaningless to speak of the new union as "adulterous" as if some rights of the previous spouse were being infringed: the former marriage, they suggest, is dead.

Unforgivable Sin

Time and again divorced Catholics ask: "Is divorce the unforgivable sin?" Unless we are making a new set of criteria for sin and forgiveness, the answer has to be No, divorce is not the unforgivable sin.

It is because the church does *not* accept the notion of "unforgivable sin" that the clear distinction is always made, at the highest level of teaching authority in the church, between something which is or is not personally sinful, and the discrepancy which may exist with the "objective status" of a person's situation in general church law.

Recent figures for Australia indicate that of marriages in which at least one partner is divorced, only three per cent take place in the Catholic church (i.e. *with* an annulment). Figures for other countries are probably similar. This seems to clearly show that for all the church's emphasis on urging Catholics to apply for annulments, the divorced Catholics who do in fact approach the tribunal are only a tiny minority. The tribunals have heavy backlogs of cases. If the numbers of applications for annulments rose greatly, the tribunals would be hopelessly clogged.

Outside the United States, where annulment processes

in many dioceses average six months, a reason which often deters Catholics from waiting until an annulment is granted before entering a second marriage is the length of time tribunal processes usually take. This is often eighteen months or more. Few people contemplating remarriage are under 30 years of age, and for a woman, the suggestion that she should wait for what may turn out to be several years can be a cause of great anxiety if there is any hope of children from the remarriage.

Speeding the Process

It is encouraging that the 1983 *New Code of Canon Law* gave guidelines to shorten the length of time taken to handle cases. In many countries, despite improvements, we are still well behind in this regard. In 1986 John Paul II urged the Roman marriage tribunal to speed up its handling of cases.

Unfortunately, to speed up the handling of cases would require a huge channeling of church resources into tribunal work. The need would be even greater if there were big numbers of new applications. Many would question the church's priorities if it redirected its finances in this way.

If the Catholic church is to be true to its founder, it bears a grave responsibility to help marriages succeed. It needs to offer marriage preparation which is of excellent standard. It should offer counseling to help those whose marriages are in trouble. These responsibilities are taken seriously in very many dioceses.

Compassion, Help, Education

But the church bears an *equally grave* responsibility to reach out with compassion and help to people whose marriages have ended, and to those who enter second marriages. In the latter instance, apart from offering the work of marriage tribunals, few dioceses I know of take these responsibilities with any seriousness at all, although the situation is improving with support for programs such as *The Beginning Experience*.

If these responsibilities are taken seriously, an improvement in the education of Catholics generally in such matters is needed. Why do so many believe that divorce is a sin? Why do people question the entire annulment process? Why do so many assume that any remarried Catholics who receive Holy Communion must be in bad conscience? There has been a failure to offer accurate knowledge in these areas. Even where a remarriage has occurred without an annulment, there may be sound reasons, recognized by the church, why a person can continue to attend the sacraments, if scandal is avoided—and scandal is not to be presumed. Very few Catholics indeed are aware of this fact.

The Eucharist is Christ's gift of himself to strengthen us in our weakness. Their belief that they are not allowed in any circumstance to receive the bread of life is one of the most serious deprivations which affects many divorced Catholics.

There is a grave obligation to offer compassion to the divorced, and accurate knowledge about divorce to all Catholics. Sadly, I still hear from many divorced Catholics of occasions when they are treated with disdain or condescension by other Catholics or have been humiliated and reduced to tears in the confessional. Yet the other

Catholics or the priests concerned probably believed they were being true to Christ over the matter.

So, it is important for us now to turn to the question: What was the attitude of Christ towards divorce, and towards the divorced?

Questions for Discussion

1. If a couple enter a second marriage before seeking an annulment from a previous marriage, is the Catholic church prepared to receive an application for an annulment from them later?
2. "Any Catholic who remarries after a divorce is living in a state of adultery." Comment.
3. "I was a divorced Catholic. Now I'm happily remarried and there's no way I could go back to my first husband, so there's no place for me in the church." Reply.
4. "I'm not a Catholic, but when I went to a priest to ask if my marriage could be annulled, the first thing he asked me was whether both of us had been baptized. It seemed odd to me. I thought he would start by asking me what went wrong with our marriage." Comment.
5. In what ways should the Catholic church and community help those who are divorced?

CHAPTER 6

Jesus and Divorce

I am never surprised at meeting divorced Catholics who believe that their divorce prevents them from receiving Holy Communion. Not too many years ago, many in their situation hardly dared attend Sunday Mass, because they felt so rejected by the Catholic community. To ask whether they were permitted to receive Holy Communion would have been a very academic question indeed, for most of them, in those days.

Any of us can conjecture about what were the reasons for those attitudes. Rejection of divorce was regarded by the church as the same as the defense of marriage. Today, a clear distinction is recognized between the two things, but those differences were overlooked.

The words of Jesus about divorce were undoubtedly basic. As we begin to consider them, however, we should bear in mind how misleading it can be to quote phrases from the Bible in isolation, without taking into account the religious and cultural circumstances in which they were written. Those who suggest that the words of the Bible are to be used as moral laws, without taking those circumstances into account, are called fundamentalists.

Jesus spoke about divorce more than once. His statements were strong, unequivocal. He condemned it. What was the context in which he spoke?

Husbands and Wives

As Mark, the writer of the earliest gospel records it, Jesus clearly disagreed with the Mosaic law permitting divorce. This is important, and well known. Less often noticed is that a central part of what Jesus very explicitly rejected was the male-centered aspect of that law, which only permitted husbands to divorce their wives. The gospel account by Mark of the words of Jesus—and also that of Luke—both make it clear that when he spoke against divorce, Jesus applied his words both ways: to husbands and to wives.

The words of Jesus condemning divorce as recorded in Matthew's gospel are similar to Mark's version, with an important, well-known exception, translated in the old versions as "except it be for adultery." A number of Christian churches in recent centuries argued that these words permit divorce on the ground of adultery. The Catholic church, refusing to take this phrase by itself as law, does not agree that these words provide authority for making adultery grounds for divorce and remarriage.

Modern scripture scholarship supports the Catholic church's view. Today's translators agree that the English word "adultery" is a mistranslation of the key Greek word *porneia* used by Matthew, which means "an uncleanness." It is not the quite different Greek word used in two other places in the same sentence to mean "adultery."

Thus the *New American Bible* translation for the entire passage in Matthew 5:31-2 reads,

It was also said, "Whoever divorces his wife must give her a bill of divorce." But I say to you, whoever divorces his wife (unless the marriage is unlawful) causes her to commit adultery, and whoever marries a divorced woman commits adultery.

If the words in brackets are omitted, this passage means virtually the same as Mark's version (Mark 10:11-12).

Not Said by Jesus

In fact, a great many scripture scholars today agree that the exception here translated as "unless the marriage is unlawful" did not come from Jesus at all. They say that Mark's version is correct: Jesus made no exceptions, and the particular words were added by Matthew, the writer of the gospel.

It is likely that Matthew had in mind various kinds of marriages, forbidden by the law of Moses as incestuous, but permitted by Roman law, under which new converts to Christianity had contracted them. An accompanying note in the *New American Bible* points out that the same problem existed in the Jewish community, where some rabbis allowed the couples to remain together. Matthew did not.

This interpretation is supported by the recent revision of the *New Jerusalem Bible*, which translates the relevant words as "except for the case of an illicit marriage." A footnote explains: "Marriage within the Jewish forbidden degrees, allowed by the Romans but not in Christianity."

Matthew apparently added this exception to the words of Jesus in order to deal with problems being encountered by the Christian communities with which he was associated, because of such converts. That this exception came from Matthew, rather than from Jesus, does not mean that it is unimportant.

The fact that Matthew felt able to add an exception to the words of Jesus, in order to meet problems Christians were encountering over marriage, suggests that while the words of Jesus on this matter were taken very seriously by the early Christians, they were not regarded as permitting no exceptions.

Pauline Privilege

This view is also supported by the very first New Testament writer who recorded the teachings of Jesus on this subject: Paul. Although our copies of the New Testament locate Paul's letters after the gospels, they were in fact written well before the gospels reached their final form. In his First Letter to the Corinthians 7:10-14, Paul quoted the condemnation of divorce by Jesus. But, making it clear that he was speaking on his own authority ("The rest is from me and not from the Lord ..."), Paul went on to make an exception which seems to predate that of Matthew. He spoke of what Catholics for a long time called the "Pauline privilege."

Referring to a marriage between two pagans, where one partner converts to Christianity and the other refuses to live at peace with the convert, Paul somewhat reluctantly, but very explicitly, permitted the new Christian to leave the pagan spouse and remarry. Throughout the centuries, Paul's exception, unlike that of Matthew, has been used in practice by the Catholic church to end some marriages. In these instances, the church gave a divorce, usually calling it a "dissolution."

In more modern times the church has permitted divorce in another comparable instance, sometimes called the

"Petrine privilege": where a marriage between an unbaptized person and a baptized member of another Christian church has ended. In certain circumstances the Catholic church will dissolve such a marriage (i.e. grant a divorce) and enable a partner to marry a Catholic in the Catholic church.

Since, reassured by Paul, it clearly recognized in practice that certain marriages—however few—could be ended, the Catholic church needed to elaborate a theology to clarify which marriages should be recognized as *not* able to be dissolved. It determined that marriages between baptized Christians (not just Catholics) are "*sacramental,*" and, once consummated by intercourse, indissoluble. When either or both partners of a marriage are unbaptized, the marriage is seen as *non-sacramental*; the couple are described as joined by "the natural bond of marriage." The church teaches that such a marriage is able to be dissolved—or a divorce granted—in certain circumstances.

The inference which the church draws, that it is sacramentality which makes the difference, is not drawn precisely from the words of Jesus—none of the people listening to Jesus had received Christian baptism. Their marriages therefore, were in these terms, non-sacramental. Rather, it is a deduction by the church, which seeks to defend marriage and to be loyal to the Savior's words.

Yet while this distinction between sacramental and non-sacramental marriages offers a clear guideline for interpreting Paul's exception, it is less satisfactory when applied to the words themselves of Jesus. His words were addressed to *unbaptized* listeners: people whose marriages the church today would regard as non-sacramental—and therefore able to be dissolved in certain circumstances. It was while speaking to those unbaptized people that Jesus condemned divorce in unequivocal terms.

For this reason, many say that there are grounds for suggesting either that Paul and Matthew (and their church communities) were wrong, and *no* exceptions should be made, or that Matthew and Paul were right, and while the words of Jesus undoubtedly reject all divorce, they express an *ideal* which the church should always aim at. In this interpretation, the words do not express a literal law, without exceptions. The church may—reluctantly—make exceptions.

How Literal?

How literally, then, should the words of Jesus be taken?

On the same and a number of other occasions Jesus presented (equally strongly, or even more emphatically) principles which the church does not feel obliged to take literally. For example, two verses earlier, Matthew records the words of Jesus about the man who looks at a woman lustfully: "If your right eye should cause you to sin, tear it out and throw it away" (verse 29). The terrifying alternative is "to have your whole body thrown into hell." The words which Jesus immediately went on to address to those who divorce were far more mild, and he made no comparable threat of hell to them. Yet the church does not want us to cut off an arm or tear out an eye. It opposes self-mutilation, and rejects the literal interpretation of the words of Jesus in that instance. It says he was using a strong image to urge us powerfully towards a goal or ideal.

Arguing in a parallel manner, some theologians suggest that when he was talking about divorce, Jesus was once again presenting an ideal. It is unquestionable that Jesus presented divorce as something to be abhorred, and to be true to his words the church today must work against divorce as much as possible. But on this matter as on others, Jesus was aware of human weakness. Paul and Matthew make clear their belief that there can be exceptions.

Prevention

Since Vatican II, the church no longer supports an approach of opposing divorce by rejecting those whose marriages have failed, but rightly urges prevention. The hope is that with good preparation for marriage, divorce will decrease. To be effective, preparation ought to be both long-term and immediate. In long-term, young people need to learn from their earliest years that marriage deserves the best and most serious preparation. Immediately: couples planning to marry should be completely convinced of this need. There should be no necessity for the priest to persuade them that they ought to make time for marriage preparation.

The church also seeks to offer the best kind of marriage counseling for any whose marriages are in difficulty. Once again, there is needed a conviction in the mind of each person that to seek counseling where problems are occurring is not a confession of failure, but is simply wise practice. Unfortunately, from my own experience as a marriage counselor I learnt that many couples delay seeking help until the problems of the marriage are almost insurmountable. It is my belief that in a number of instances, had they sought help earlier, the problems could have been healed.

The Divorced

What of those whose marriages have ended in divorce?

It seems beyond doubt to me that in the past the church—and that means all of us—sinned grievously against these unfortunate people. No matter that the church's intention was to defend marriage: the divorced experienced rejection and what can only be described as *effective* excommunication.

By contrast, we have the opposite example from Jesus. Despite the strength of his condemnation of divorce, when he met a (many times) divorced woman at Jacob's well in Samaria, she found no rejection from him at all. Rather the reverse: he offered her warmth and acceptance, even though, as Jesus pointed out to her, she had been married five times, and was at present living in a *de facto* relationship. He chose her to be the means through whom her entire village was converted. Read the account in John 4:5-42.

As a church, our attitude towards divorce has been based too greatly on a legalistic interpretation of the words of Jesus, and too little on his example.

I would like to conclude by summarizing some major points, and suggesting some further reading.

- Jesus clearly opposed divorce, but did not reject the divorced person: instead he offered compassion.
- Divorce itself is not a sin, and a divorced person (not remarried) has every right to continue to receive Holy Communion.
- Paul strongly urged the faithful to observe the words of Jesus regarding the permanence of marriage. However, he did not hesitate to offer the possibility of divorce and remarriage in one particular situation. Matthew took the same attitude. The church, basing itself on the authority of Paul, has continued to urge the observance of the words of Jesus, but allows exceptions, permitting divorce and remarriage in certain circumstances. It has extended the exceptions Paul allowed.

- The church sees sacramental, consummated marriages as indissoluble. However, it now has a marriage tribunal system in which questions can be raised about whether the *consent* on which the marriage was based was lacking in some essential way. If this lack is established, remarriage in the Catholic church is permitted. In the last thirty years or so, it has extended very considerably the grounds on which annulments may be granted. It could do so again.
- Where a case cannot be proved—for lack of witnesses, for instance—but the person feels convinced that the marriage was not valid, the church fully respects a conscience decision to remarry, although it will not publicly authorize the remarriage. It recognizes the right of such a remarried person to receive Holy Communion in good conscience, scandal being avoided.
- There is less clear support by the church for a person who is in a doubtful state of conscience about the validity of a first marriage when there is a remarriage. However, the complexity of the church's annulment procedures may at the present time make it difficult for a person to overcome this doubt. There is need for better communication in this area, as in others.

This is where Catholic church teaching and practice stands at the present time. It is certainly changing and developing, but if we base our approach on both the words *and example* of Jesus, we need have no fear.

Questions for Discussion

1. What are the best ways for the Catholic church to show that it believes that marriages should be indissoluble, as Jesus said?

2. "Don't you Catholics believe in the Bible? Our church follows what Jesus said, and permits remarriage after divorce if there was adultery." Reply.
3. "My boyfriend and I are planning to get married. How can we make sure our marriage doesn't end in divorce?" Reply.
4. "My wife and I are having a lot of fights, and she wants to go to a counselor, but I said, 'What can they tell you? We'll work it out for ourselves.'" Reply.
5. What can we learn from the example of Jesus with the woman at the well?

Afterword

"But why haven't we been told this before?"

The woman sounded angry, accusing. I had been giving a talk on annulments to a group of Solo Parents, and during discussion I had spoken about the possibility of making a decision in good conscience about one's first marriage and going to Holy Communion. I have been asked her question many times, but it was still difficult to answer.

It became even more difficult when I spoke to her privately afterwards, and she told me some of her story as each of us held a polystyrene cup of coffee. Her first marriage had lasted about six months. Two years later she remarried to a fine man in a Presbyterian church ceremony. That was ten years ago. Early last year, wishing to return to the practice of her religion, she applied for an annulment of the first marriage and her case was at an advanced stage. I had to say to her that she could hardly have better grounds for believing that her first marriage had not been valid—the tribunal was obviously taking the case very seriously indeed.

"Do you mean to say that I could have been going to

Holy Communion all this time, and no one told me?"

I felt embarrassed. That was what I did mean.

Another problem was raised in a letter which I received from Western Australia following on the series of articles in *Annals Australia* on which the present book was based. The writer said that she firmly believed that the first marriage of her husband could not have been valid, and that the conditions for her to make a good conscience decision, and go to Holy Communion were present. But how, she asked, was she to explain this in confession?

As I tried to explain in my reply, Catholic teaching is that the Sacrament of Reconciliation is for confession of our *sins*. But a decision made in good conscience is not, "I am doing something sinful but there are reasons which permit me to receive Holy Communion." In general, then, the marital situation of a person who has taken a conscience decision is not something that needs to be brought up in the confessional, although there are a hundred ways in which any of us can fail in God's sight and obviously we should confess any serious sins we may have committed.

In fact, it is less than fair to a priest, and a misunderstanding of the conditions which apply to a conscience decision, to present to him for approval during a brief confession a personal decision taken after lengthy consideration of the vast range of complex factors in a marriage breakdown. As indicated above in the explanation of the conditions, the conscience decision is one which is to be taken *by the person concerned*: one does not proceed on the basis that "Father X said it was all right." On the other hand priests—"pastors of souls"—should be able to help people know about it and understand what the decision means.

See *Bibliography* for further reading on these and other matters discussed already.

APPENDIX I

When Dreams Die

This statement was first issued by the bishops of New Zealand in 1982, and then, in their own name, by the bishops of Australia.

The Pastoral Care of Separated and Divorced Catholics

Hope and joy are born of compassion. The compassionate show the face of God to a world in which sadness, doubt and fear afflict so many.

Hope and joy are the promise and gift which the Father holds out to his much loved creation. To be compassionate, to be givers of that hope and joy, is the call of the Lord Jesus to all who follow his way.

Because we are convinced of this, and because we want to proclaim our own hope and joy in the risen Jesus, we write to you, the Catholic faithful, concerning those of our fellow Catholics who are suffering the pain and loss of marriage breakdown.

These Catholic brothers and sisters can very easily feel "left out" and even somehow "second class" when their fellow Catholics are hesitant about befriending, maintaining contact and making a place in parish life for them.

This hesitancy, sometimes felt as coldness, may be due to embarrassment or a false sensitivity to the situation.

But it may also come about from the mistaken idea that these people have somehow sinned. This need not be so. Marital separation or civil divorce alone do not mean estrangement from the church.

Belonging

The church's teaching on the indissolubility and fidelity of marriage needs to be seen alongside her teaching on the need for compassion and understanding towards those in any kind of difficulty. We want our people to understand this, so that the separated and divorced have a sure sense of belonging, and feel encouraged to participate in the sacramental life of the Catholic community.

Pope John Paul II, in his 1981 statement on "The Christian Family in the Modern World," placed this two-fold teaching in beautiful perspective when he wrote:

> As a mutual gift of two persons, this intimate union, as well as the good of children, imposes total fidelity on the spouses and argues for an unbreakable oneness between them ...
>
> To bear witness to the inestimable value of the indissolubility and fidelity of marriage is one of the most precious and urgent tasks of Christian couples in our time (para 20).
>
> I earnestly call upon pastors and the whole community of the faithful to help the divorced, and with solicitous care to make sure that they do not consider themselves as separated from the church, for as baptized persons they can, and indeed must, share in her life ... Let the church pray for them, encourage them and show herself a merciful mother, and thus sustain them in faith and hope (para 84).

We wish to emphasize that, for their part, separated

and divorced Catholics are among those who most strongly affirm the church's teaching on marriage. The breaking of their marriage can serve to emphasize, for them, the quality, dignity and strength that are found only in the permanence and faithfulness of marriage.

Crippling Effects

With divorce becoming increasingly accepted in our society, there is a danger we may become uninterested in, or insensitive to the effects of divorce on the lives of those caught up in it. We cannot let familiarity minimize the significance of these effects, which can be crippling and emotionally destructive.

Increased tolerance of the facts of divorce does not lessen its pain for those involved. It is therefore particularly opportune and important that our church community affirms its commitment to those made more vulnerable by the trauma of marriage breakdown.

Death of a Dream

We must avoid the false idea that divorce is always chosen as an easy way out. Separation and divorce mark the death of a dream, and dreams die when hope no longer holds meaning.

The result is grief.

Further, for those whose marriage began as a life-commitment, there is the realization that a solemn promise has been broken. So inevitably there will be feelings of guilt.

Grief and guilt collide in the personality of the separated

or divorced person, resulting in a loneliness that some find intolerable.

A person is torn from someone who had been accepted as a life-partner—someone with whom they had hoped and even planned to share all the challenges of living together. Both people still exist, but their life together has died.

This death has been termed "psychological widowhood"—a situation that can, of course, also occur in existing marriages.

The stress and sense of loss which accompany and follow psychological widowhood can be compared with the reactions to separation through physical death.

This is true also for the children.

Their tragedy is often greater. Their pain, which they cannot easily identify or understand, is submerged in the confusion of being "caught in between" in the chaos of separation. Bereavement—in its literal sense of loss—leaves orphans.

A Time for Grieving ... and Forgiving

We wish now to address ourselves particularly to all of you involved in the heartbreak of marriage death.

We recognize that there is a real grief process that you have to work through. There may also be a deep anger compounding the hurt you feel. Both your grief and your anger should meet a compassionate response within the community of the church.

The church is uniquely placed to help you face your anger and find the courage to forgive, for the church knows that forgiveness—the reconciling love of Jesus Christ—is the foundation of her hope. Anger damages the one who is angry. Like grief it must be enabled to heal.

You should not have to apologize for seeking the counsel of the priest. On the contrary, you should find in the priest a ready listener and an understanding pastor.

Jesus, the Good Shepherd, speaks through those who have committed their lives to his service when he says, "Come to me all you who labor and are heavily burdened, and I will give you rest . . . for I am gentle and humble in heart" (Matthew 11:28).

Likewise, the parish community should reflect the warmth of a loving family. When the parish opens its arms in welcome and love to touch the disadvantaged, it embraces Jesus (cf. Matthew 25:31-46).

You must know that your burden of loneliness does not have to be carried alone. The Lord who is close to the broken-hearted (Ps. 34) wants you to find peace. It is for the community that bears His name to reveal the resting place of peace.

Life Needs Love

Much of what we have shared here also applies to those who, after divorce, have attempted marriage outside the church. We want to add a special word for you.

While it is not possible for you, who have divorced and remarried, to celebrate the sacraments as full members of the worshiping community, that community has an important obligation to support, encourage and nourish your faith. You remain our brothers and sisters.

Three years ago, in his first letter to the church and to all men and women of goodwill, Pope John Paul reminded us that life is impossible without love. If love is not revealed to us, if we do not encounter love, "experience it and participate intimately in it," then living is "senseless" (cf. para 10, "Redeemer of Man").

These words have special relevance here. Personal faults

invariably contribute to any marriage breakdown. No one denies that persons can fail. But, if we understand that failure does not make a person unlovable in the eyes of God, it will be clear that, whatever their failures, people always have a right to our love.

The need for love does not disappear simply because a person may no longer be married. Having known love, the need is even greater. If love is not shown by an accepting, open, humble and spiritually adult Christian community, it may well be sought in a new irregular friendship. We all have a responsibility here.

- We urge you who are remarried to examine your particular circumstances and, if your pastor so advises, seek the help of the diocesan matrimonial tribunal.
- We ask our priests, teachers and lay ministers to study the church's teaching on marriage, to actively support people who are trying to help, and to be ready to listen to and gently guide those seeking advice.
- Our Catholic Social Services offer professional counseling and guidance. An introduction to these services, when a difficulty is first recognized, may help couples avoid later crisis.
- Parish pastoral councils should take a special interest in this vital area, looking for ways in which the liturgical, social and educational welfare of those with marriage difficulties can be enriched.

Vocation

But the separated and divorced are not expected to be mere recipients of support. They themselves have a part to play in the life of the community. Indeed many, from the experience of their own suffering, are already ministering to fellow parishioners trying to cope with their marriage relationships.

We applaud this Christlike concern, itself a sign of faithfulness. We feel sure that you, who have been victims of marriage breakdown, are called to share your courage and faith with those who find themselves on a similar journey.

Mercy

All of us, sharing in the priesthood of Jesus by reason of our baptism, are to minister to one another in love characterized by mercy. Mercy is the unifying and elevating power that makes compassion possible. Pope John Paul, in his timely letter "Rich in Mercy," writes that this love means "the cordial tenderness and sensitivity so eloquently spoken of in the parable of the prodigal son, and also in the parables of the lost sheep and the lost coin . . . it is indispensable in pastoral work" (para 14).

Be especially respectful of the conscience and convictions of one another. Be careful not to impose excessive burdens, not to further isolate those already alone, not to allow our own ignorance or prejudice to block the uplifting, healing power of the Holy Spirit (cf. "The Evangelization of Peoples," Pope Paul VI, 1975, para 79).

In reaching out to our separated, divorced and remarried Catholics, we offer an assurance that you are loved. If your present difficulties sometimes seem insoluble, we pray that the care with which you are held in your respective parish communities will be the seed of hope and joy in your own lives, and that you will find peace. The soothing touch of Jesus comes in the spirit of hospitality which, ideally, enlivens every parish.

Compassion—Not Pity

When Jesus asks his followers to "be compassionate as your Father is compassionate" (Luke 6:36), he asks that we stand alongside the troubled and distressed, to take some of the weight of their burden and to help them again lift up their heads and their hearts.

Compassion has little to do with pity, or simply feeling sorry for the other. It is a freely offered and active sharing in whatever suffering the other is enduring. Such a sharing, which is always careful not to force itself on the privacy of the sufferer, brings hope and joy, for it restores a sense of belonging to the person alone and afraid.

Compassion becomes more tangible, and consequently more possible, when each of us acknowledges the need of God's patient, tender and merciful love in our own lives. Then, encouraged by the unspeakable richness of God's own compassion, "with our unrest, uncertainty and even our weakness and sinfulness, with our life and our death" ("Redeemer of Man," para 10), we will encourage one another and so draw nearer to Christ, our lasting hope and joy.

APPENDIX II

The Beginning Experience

The Beginning Experience is an outstanding program to help people experiencing the grief of a divorce or the death of a spouse. On a live-in weekend, it invites them to deal with grief and, putting the past behind, to look forward to the future with renewed hope and confidence. There are follow-up programs to help continue the process. Although Catholic in origin it is available to people of other religions or of no religion.

The program is widely available throughout the English-speaking world, including the United States, Canada, United Kingdom, Ireland, Australia, New Zealand and Singapore. A Hispanic edition is also available.

More precise contact information about *The Beginning Experience* in these countries may be obtained from the International Ministry Center at the following address:

The Beginning Experience
International Ministry Center
305 Michigan Ave
Detroit MI 48226 Ph. 313-965-5110
USA Fax 313-237-4644

At the local level, information about coming Beginning Experience weekends is also usually obtainable from the Catholic Family Welfare, or Centacare, or Catholic Social Services of the local diocese.

APPENDIX III

The Rainbows Program

The writer is convinced that too little help has been available in the past for children affected by marriage breakdown. *Rainbows* is an excellent program designed for children from single-parent and step-families, aged from pre-school to university level, to help them come to terms with their situation. The program runs primarily in schools, but may also be offered in other centers. Religious and secular versions are available. The secondary school version is called *Spectrum*.

Contact Address:

Rainbows
1111 Tower Rd
Schaumburg IL 60173 — Ph. 708-310-1880
USA — Fax 708-310-0120

Information may be obtained from this address regarding the availability of *Rainbows* in the following countries: Australia, Austria, Canada, Ireland, New Zealand, Singapore, South Africa, the United Kingdom and the United States.

APPENDIX

III

[illegible]

[illegible]

Bibliography

Gerald D. Coleman, *Divorce and Remarriage in the Catholic Church*, New York, Paulist Press, 1988

Bernard Haring, *No Way Out? Pastoral Care of the Divorced and Remarried*, Middlegreen, St Paul, 1989

Harville Hendrix, *Getting the Love You Want. A Guide for Couples*, New York, Henry Holt, 1988

John Hosie, *Before You Love Again: Starting a Successful New Relationship*, Sydney, Millennium Books, 1993

Kevin T. Kelly, *Divorce and Second Marriage: Facing the Challenge*, London, Collins, 1982

Mel Krantzler, *Learning to Love Again*, New York, Crowell, 1977

Roderick Phillips, *Untying the Knot: A Short History of Divorce*, Cambridge, Cambridge University Press, 1991

Geoffrey Robinson, *Marriage, Divorce and Nullity: A Guide to the Annulment Process in the Catholic Church*, Melbourne, Collins Dove, 1984

Judith Wallerstein and Sandra Blakeslee, *Second Chances: Men, Women and Children a Decade After Divorce*, New York, Ticknor and Fields, 1989

James J. Young, ed., *Ministering to the Divorced Catholic*, New York, Paulist Press, 1979

Index